Written by Margaret Snyder

Illustrated by Mario Cortes and The Thompson Brothers

MERRIGOLD PRESS • NEW YORK

Once upon a time there was a lovely peasant girl named Minderella. Minderella worked terribly hard for the nasty Duke Donald and his three very spoiled nephews, Huey, Dewey, and Louie.

"Minderella! Minderella! Iron my shirt," ordered Huey.

"Minderella! Minderella! Wash my pants," demanded Dewey.

"Minderella! Minderella! Shine my shoes," shouted Louie.

All day long they ordered her about. The rest of the time they ate and slept.

One day, while the nephews were sunning themselves on the lawn, Sir Goofy, one of the King's noblemen, arrived at the house.

"Prince Mickey is having a pool party this evening," he announced. "Everyone in the kingdom is invited. How many will be attending from the Duke's house?" he asked.

"Four," answered the Duke.

"And the lady makes five?" Sir Goofy asked, looking at Minderella. Duke Donald pointed to an enormous mound of dirty laundry. "Minderella can't go," he scoffed. "She has to finish the laundry tonight."

That evening, as Minderella scrubbed clothes, she watched the Duke and his nephews leave for the party. "Good-bye, Minderella," they teased.

"Remember, if you want to go swimming, you can always jump into the washtub!"

Minderella scrubbed harder and harder when all of a sudden a carriage arrived. "Now who could this be?" she wondered.

A coachman opened the door for the tall stranger. "Hello! I'm Clarabelle, your dairy godmother."

Minderella was stunned. "I didn't know I had a dairy godmother," she said.

Clarabelle laughed and took Minderella by the hand. "Now, my dear—how come you're not ready to go to Prince Mickey's pool party?" she asked.

"I have to finish the laundry," Minderella answered softly.

"Nonsense!" said Clarabelle. "I'll finish the laundry while you go to the party."

Minderella's heart soared. Then it sank. "But, Dairy Godmother!" Minderella cried. "I have nothing to wear to a royal pool party."

Clarabelle smiled. "Ah! That's just what dairy godmothers are for!" she said. She waved her magic wand and—*poof*—Minderella was dressed in a beautiful bathing suit, bathing cap, and robe, with a pair of goggles in her hand. On her feet were a wonderful pair of glass flippers. "Oh, Dairy Godmother! How beautiful!" Minderella exclaimed.

"Pluto, my coachman, will drive you to the party," Clarabelle said. "But you must be back here by the stroke of midnight!"

"Oh, I will," promised Minderella.

When the carriage reached the palace, Pluto escorted Minderella up to the gate. The party was even more wonderful than Minderella had imagined. Colorful lanterns lit up the night. There were music and flowers and strolling minstrels. Clutching her precious glass flippers, Minderella made her way through the crowd. Sir Goofy was announcing a swim race. "The winner will be awarded one bag of gold," he said.

"A bag of gold!" Minderella thought. "That could be my chance to leave my job at the Duke's house and start a new life!"

Sometime later Sir Goofy announced, "Prince Mickey's swim race is about to begin." Minderella dashed around the pool and got in line with the other contestants. Duke Donald and his nephews wondered who was the lovely stranger in her bathing cap and goggles.

Minderella took off her robe and slipped into her glass flippers. Her swimming suit and flippers sparkled. Prince Mickey stared. "Who's *that*?" he asked Sir Goofy.

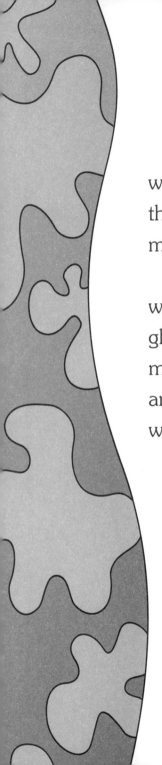

Sir Goofy promised to find out as soon as the race was over. Then he walked to the pool's edge to start the race. "May the best swimmer win. On your marks, get set, go!"

With a powerful dive, Minderella sprang into the water and started swimming with all her might. Her glass flippers propelled her through the water like magic! When she reached the other side of the pool and looked behind her, she saw that she was the winner!

Sir Goofy helped Minderella out of the pool and was about to award her the bag of gold when the clock in the tower began to strike midnight. "Oh, no!" Minderella cried. "I've got to go!" She took off her flippers and raced through the gate.

Prince Mickey chased after her. "Your prize!" he shouted. "Come back!" But Minderella had disappeared from sight.

As Prince Mickey headed back into the palace, he spotted something shiny on the ground. The mystery guest had dropped one of her glass flippers!

"Come quickly, Sir Goofy," he called. "We're going to search the kingdom for the maiden whose foot fits this flipper!" Prince Mickey and Sir Goofy jumped into the royal carriage and raced off into the night.

As soon as Minderella had hidden her glass flipper under her bed, she heard a knock on the door. There were Prince Mickey and Sir Goofy, holding her missing glass flipper and the bag of gold. "Will you try this on?" Sir Goofy politely asked. "We're looking for the winner of this bag of gold."

Minderella sat down excitedly and tried on the flipper. Just then Duke Donald and his nephews burst into the room!

"That's ours!" Duke Donald shouted, and he snatched the flipper away from Minderella.

First Duke Donald insisted that the flipper belonged to Huey, and then to Dewey, and then to Louie, but it did not fit any of them.

"Please excuse me for a moment," said Minderella politely as she left the room. When she reappeared, she was wearing the other glass flipper.

"You're the winner of the swimming race," Prince Mickey exclaimed. Then he took Minderella by the hand to give her the bag of gold. As Prince Mickey gazed into Minderella's eyes, he knew he would never again meet anyone as sweet and as polite and as brave—and as great a swimmer—as Minderella.

A few months later, Sir Goofy announced that Prince Mickey and Minderella were getting married. On the day of their wedding, everyone in the kingdom was invited to celebrate.

Well, *almost* everyone. Duke Donald Duck and his nephews couldn't come to the party because they were too busy at home doing their own laundry.